T... Your Life By Renewing Your Mind

Using the Word of GOD to Change Your Life!

T.A. Williams

Holy Fire Publishing
Oak Ridge, TN

Published by:
Holy Fire Publishing
P.O. Box 5192, Oak Ridge, TN 37831-5192
www.christianpublish.com

ISBN: 0-9761112-0-9

Printed in the United States of America and the United Kingdom

Dedication

This book is dedicated to my father & mother, the late Johnnie, Sr. and Alberta, without whom I would not be the man that I am today.

And to my brother, the late Johnnie Williams Jr. who went home to be with the Lord before this book was completed.

Contents

Introduction

Romans 12:2
And be not conformed to this world: but be ye transformed
by the renewing of your mind, that ye may prove what [is]
that good, and acceptable, and perfect, will of God.

THINGS WILL CHANGE IN YOUR LIFE WHEN YOU BEGIN TO CHANGE THE WAY YOU THINK ABOUT THEM!

Often, there are times when two or more people experience the same events in life yet one person responds totally different to the situation than the others. Why is that? I believe it's because that person has simply changed the way they will look at the situation. You could have two people go through financial difficulties, marriage problems, problems with their kids or even problems on the job. While one person blows up and totally reacts to the situation(s), the other person is able to go about their daily routine as if nothing externally is wrong. It's not that they are ignoring the situation hoping that it goes away. They, like many other believers, understand that everything is either GOD sent or GOD allowed to make us better, so they do not allow the vicissitudes of life drag them down. Their situation is changed because they have changed the way they think about things.

There's a reason that Paul so eloquently states in II Corinthians 10: 4 & 5 that "The weapons of our warfare are not carnal, but mighty through GOD to pulling down of strongholds; casting down imaginations and every high thing that exalteth itself against the knowledge of GOD, and bringing into captivity every thought to the obedience of Christ". GOD had revealed to Paul that the battle he and other Christians were going to surly fight would be fought in their minds, not a normal field of battle. GOD knows that if the devil can control your mind and the way you think about things, he will win the battle for your soul. This is why Paul wrote about the tearing down of "strongholds". Strongholds are wrong thoughts and perceptions, which contradict the true knowledge of GOD and His ways. Ignorance and misunderstanding of GOD and His ways will bind you more strongly than any chains. The lack of knowledge the world has regarding GOD and His ways is what's keeping many people bound in hopelessness, despair, anxiety and stress. This is why Paul told the Romans *Be not conformed to this world*.

The opposite of being *conformed* to this world is being *transformed* by the renewing of your mind. The battle ground between an evil conformity and a good transformation is within your mind. Thus if you truly want to change things around in your life, you must begin the process of transforming your mind or changing the way you look at situations. Your life or situation will not change simply by making some external adjustments. You can change your hair, change jobs, or even move to a different city; it does not matter. Your situation will not change until you begin the process of strengthening your "inner man" and changing your way of thinking. It's too easy to have external conduct that looks good, but an inward life and manner of thinking that is backwards and offensive to GOD.

It is my prayer that as you read this devotional and meditate on the scriptures that I've used for each day, that you'll begin the glorious transformation of your life that will come by simply changing the way you view the things that are happening in your life. One of the most important scriptures to me as I began my journey to a renewed mind, and one that I urge you to read & seriously think about, is Hebrews 11:40. As you begin your transformation, the words that Paul chose in the entire 11th chapter of Hebrews will be very important. We all know that the chapter begins by giving us the definitive definition of faith ("*Now faith is the substance of things hoped for, the evidence of things not seen*), and it goes on to give us many examples of how faith enabled many people in the Bible to overcome various situations that they encountered in life. They all had different circumstances that they encountered but they all had one thing in common: faith.

The definition and the examples of faith are all very good and useful, but it was my coming to an understanding of the words Paul used to end the 11th chapter that truly helped me to tie the entire meaning of the chapter together. Your getting an understanding of this will be of vital importance as you begin to transform your life by renewing your mind. The 40th verse of the 11th chapter begins by telling us that "*GOD having provided some better thing for us…*" Understanding this is important because you'll begin to realize that GOD wouldn't take you through all that you're going through to give you something less that what you already have! Coming to that realization alone may be the key to transforming someone's life.

It was not my intention to write a book when I began to write how, through studying the word of GOD, I began to have a different understanding of the things that I was experiencing. I began to realize through the scriptures that it's the things that we go through that best prepare us for where GOD is ultimately going to take us. I began to fully understand that all things work together for good to those that love the Lord and are the called according to His purpose. It may not seem like it at the time but GOD will use what we might think is a very traumatic event to get us to where He has called us to be. It may not feel good, it may not seemingly make any sense to you but GOD knows where He's going to take you and all that He must expose you to in order to get you to that place.

I pray that something that I've written in the pages that follow will be a blessing to you and will give you a new perspective on the things that you are experiencing right now in life. I believe that GOD has to take us through transformation before we are fully prepared for the elevation that He has promised us in His word.

DAY 1

IT'S TIME TO CHANGE YOUR PERSPECTIVE!

Read: II Corinthians 4: 16 –18
"For our light affliction, which is but for a moment, worketh for us a far more exceeding and eternal weight of glory:
While we look not at the things which are seen, but at the things which are not seen: for the things which are seen are temporal: but the things which are not seen are eternal."

As we begin the process of transforming our lives, we have to first remember that the very first step in this process is to re-evaluate how we are looking at the things that GOD allows to happen in our lives and begin to change our perspectives with regards to those situations. During the many uncertain times that we all will face in life, often the only thing that holds some of us together is that we are able to keep things in the proper perspective. Some of us are so filled with the word of GOD that regardless of the things that we are facing, we hold onto the word that Paul wrote in Romans 8:28 *"And we know that all things work together for good to them that love GOD and are the called according to His purpose."* Your understanding of the two very important words in this scripture, "all things", will be the beginning of your transformation journey. Taken at face value, "all things" means GOD uses everything good, bad or seemingly unrelated to get us to where He is trying to take us. It is the devils job to try and deceive us with problems and get us to think that GOD is not with us during our struggles. But that could not be farther from the truth.

Our success in life often has less to do with our abilities than it does with our perspectives. If we continue to look at things the wrong way long enough, no matter how talented you are, you will miss your mark. If you don't begin to fully understand what you are going through, why you are going through it, and how you should go through you will forever be frustrated and defeated living well below the levels that GOD intends for you to live. Trying to help others gain this understanding is my reason for writing this book and in II Corinthians 4: 16 & 18, Paul shows us the following three important facts about our perspective:

1. *Never lose heart, progress isn't always visible!*
Although things on the outside seem to be going astray, we have the assurance that GOD is using these things to strengthen and renew us day after day. Too often we tend to focus our minds only on the things

that we can see with our eyes, regardless of how many scriptures tell us to do just the opposite. Our eyes will often fool us because the things that we think we see are not always what they appear to be. For example, you're driving down a country road and pass a large field. This field is a couple of acres in size but you don't see (with your eyes) any crops growing, so you begin to think that this field is just going to waste. But, if you truly want to transform your life, you have to look at "fields" like this in your life and begin to realize that just because you don't see any crops doesn't mean that the seeds haven't been planted…the harvest just hasn't come up yet!

2. *Our struggles are developing us!*

You must know that GOD has a tendency to use the things that we are going through to develop us and get us to the point where we are able to bring forth much fruit in our lives and, as Jesus says in John 15:16, He wants our fruit to remain. It is not a blessing if GOD continues to open things up to you but you are not able to maintain the blessing that He has given you. Often, it's what you have to go through to get something that will make you more conscience of it's value, and in turn, do whatever is necessary to maintain it. That is how GOD uses our struggles. Struggles are there to develop us and get us to the point where we are in full appreciation of the blessings of GOD when He releases them in our lives and thus do all to maintain them.

3. *Fix your eyes on the invisible!*

If we are to truly transform our lives, we must remember that as Christians, we should not fix our eyes on victories that are visible to the human eye. If you've lived a while, you know that a lot of the challenging situations that you have faced in life have been short lived. It may have seemed like you were going through it for a long time but in actuality, it was just a temporary situation. The key to success is this, do not make permanent decisions over temporary situations! You will find out that the only thing that remains constant in your life is Christ and if you fix your eyes on Him and the things that are eternal, He will see you through all of your tough times. As Paul states in the 17th verse, *"Our light affliction, which is but for a moment, worketh for us a far more exceeding and eternal weight of glory"*. If you embrace that one
verse, you will be able to handle all of the situations that you face in life.

Remember:

The importance of the blessings that await us in the eternal realm, far exceed the ones visible to the human eye. If you allow Him to, GOD will develop your perspective so that you will not be driven solely by the things that you see.

WHY!

READ: Genesis 25:22
"And the children struggled together within her; and she said, if it be so, why am I thus? And she went to enquire of the Lord."

Like many of us, Rebekah (with the help of Isaac) asked the Lord to bless her in ways that she could never have performed on her own. For she was technically barren but desired to have a child, so Isaac and Rebekah prayed for a child. A funny thing happened though between their initial prayers and when they actually came into their blessing. Rebekah went through some really tough times during her pregnancy; so much so that she was led to wonder "if this is actually a good thing and an answer to my prayers Lord, why am I going through all of this mess?" Does this sound familiar to anyone?

Personally, there have been times in my life that I have had to ask GOD things like "If this job is a blessing from you, why am I going through all of these problems?" or "GOD, if this is where you want me to be, why are things so difficult?" I believe that it's human nature for us to think that just because

GOD blesses us that means that we will not go through some trials and tests in our lives. But the scriptures tell us that "Many are the afflictions of the righteous, but the Lord delivereth him out of them all." It is the things that we have to go through that develop us into the Christians that GOD is calling us to be. Although it's difficult to understand initially, once you do, you begin to walk and talk differently because you understand that it is all a part of the process.

Take a woman, like Rebekah, who gets pregnant. It would be silly for her to feel that something is wrong simply because she begins to have morning sickness and she starts gaining weight. These are simply the things that she has to go through to realize her blessing. Too often when we are faced with trials and tests, we are too willing to give up because we think "this couldn't be GOD's will because, if it were, I wouldn't be going through this." Some of us fail to realize that it's through these tests that GOD develops us and gets us prepared for the blessing and everything else that goes along with it.

Remember:
Instead of asking GOD "Why?", understand that if you ask GOD to show up and show out in your life,

you should EXPECT some sort of test that will be sent to prepare you for the blessing that you've asked for.

Day 3

Overcoming Life's Difficulties

Read: I John 5: 4 & 5

"For whatsoever is born of God overcometh the world: and this is the victory that overcometh the world, our faith.
Who is he that overcometh the world, but he that believeth that Jesus is the Son of God?"

It's a great thing to realize that GOD has not kept a bunch of secrets from us? He has told us that while on this "yellow brick road" of life, we will (not might) experience troubles. Disease will afflict bodies. Divorce will break hearts. Death will make widows and devastation will destroy countries. We shouldn't expect anything less. But just because troubles come our way and begin to wreck havoc in our lives doesn't mean that we should panic. The above scriptures tell us that since we are believers, we are guaranteed victory over the world.

Jesus said in John 16:33 *"In the world ye shall have tribulation: but be of good cheer; I have overcome the world."* We must know and believe that GOD is using today's difficulties to strengthen us for tomorrow. GOD is equipping us for our journey. The key is to constantly remind ourselves that whatever is going on in our lives is either GOD sent or GOD allowed, so it must be a part of His development plan for our lives. Also, and this is important, remember that because you believe that Jesus is the Son of GOD, it is guaranteed that you will be victorious over any attack that may come your way!

Remember:
Victory is guaranteed because you believe!

Day 4

Discovering GOD in the Storm

Read: Matthew 7: 24 – 27
"Therefore whosoever heareth these sayings of mine, and doeth them, I will liken him unto a wise man, which built his house upon a rock:
And the rain descended, and the floods came, and the winds blew, and beat upon that house; and it fell not: for it was founded upon a rock.
And every one that heareth these sayings of mine, and doeth them not, shall be likened unto a foolish man, which built his house upon the sand:
And the rain descended, and the floods came, and the winds blew, and beat upon that house; and it fell: and great was the fall of it."

There are many things that the storms in our lives come to teach us. I would like to point out three things that we must understand about storms and three things we will discover while in our storms:

Three Things about Storms
- *Storms Will Come* - they are opportunities for GOD to show up in our lives. GOD's strength is made perfect in our weaknesses and the storms of life expose our weaknesses.

- *Storms Don't Last Forever* - they are sent our way for a short period of time; we determine how long they stay in our lives. We have a tendency to talk about the storm and dwell on it long after it's over. While we're going through the storm, we have to deal with the winds & the waves. Then, after the storm, we continually talk about how bad the storm was and how much we had to go through during the storm. We must learn how to put the storm behind us and enjoy the sunshine that is before us!

- *Make Sure That You're Prepared for the Storm* – if you know that it's going to storm, make sure that you're carrying an umbrella. In the scripture, the storm came to both houses. The difference was simply that the wise man built his house in anticipation of the storm (on the word of GOD), and because the foolish man did not prepare for the inevitable storm, when the winds and waves beat upon his house, great was it's fall.

Three Discoveries in the Storm

- *The Purpose of the Storm* – Don't waste your time trying to avoid the storm. It's through the storms of life that GOD is preparing you for where he's eventually going to take you. There is a predetermined path that GOD has for each of us, and that path includes not only the good things that we will experience in life, but also the storms that we must endure.

- *The Power in the Storm* – GOD will challenge you to your destiny. Put another way, GOD is using the trials and tribulations of life to move you towards your predetermined destiny!

- *The Presence of GOD in the Storm* – Psalms 46:1 tells us that GOD is a *"very present help IN TROUBLE"* or in our storms. In the 14th chapter of Matthew, Jesus showed up and proved how mighty he was. See, if you trust GOD during your storms, like Peter, you'll be able to do things that others have said was impossible. That's the type of faith that GOD expects for us to have. This is why Jesus admonished Peter in Matthew 14:31 saying *"O, ye of little faith, why didst thou doubt?"* Know that even when you're going through storms, GOD has got your back!

Remember:
Storms will come and storms will go. And your ability to receive GOD's promises is determined by your ability to believe GOD's promises.

Day 5

GOD Has Got Your Back!

Read: II Peter 2:9
"...the Lord knows how to rescue GODLY people from their trials..." (New Living Translation)

Have you ever wondered how you came out of situations that took other people out? When the presence of GOD is on something, that thing can be on fire but it will not be consumed (Exodus 3:2). GOD's presence in our lives guarantees that, not only will you not be consumed by the fire that you're in, but His presence also guarantees that HE will bring you out of the fire eventually. Psalms 34:19 tells us that *"Many are the afflictions of the righteous but GOD delivers them out of them all."* The key word here is ALL. Not some of them, not most of them but all of your afflictions GOD says HE will deliver you out from them.

So while we are guaranteed to go through many afflictions in our lives, if we keep our faith & trust in GOD and concentrate on Him during our afflictions, He promises that He will have your back. Revelations 2:10 instructs us in this way, *"Fear none of those things which thou shalt suffer...be thou faithful unto death and I will give thee a crown of life.*" There will be many troubling situations that we all must endure, but through the vicissitudes of life (the dictionary defines vicissitudes as "one of the sudden or unexpected changes or shifts often encountered in one's life, activities or surroundings) it is important that we understand that GOD has our backs and that He is a *"rewarder of them that diligently seek Him"* (Hebrews 11:6).

Remember: Even during those times when things seem to be at their worst, GOD is able to deliver you from all of your troubles.

Day 6

GOD Uses Unlikely People!

Read: Judges 6: 15 & 16
"And he said unto him, Oh my Lord, wherewith shall I save Israel? Behold, my family is poor in Manasseh, and I am the least in my father's house.
And the Lord said unto him, Surely I will be with thee, and thou shalt smite the Midianites as one man."

In this society, we are often consumed with accomplishing goals and positioning ourselves within organizations so that when opportunities for advancement come, we'd be considered the "obvious" choice. The networking, working late hours, and trying to get to know the "right" people are just some of the things we do to make people feel that we are the most qualified person for the job. But we serve a GOD who has throughout scriptures used the most unlikely people to fulfill His purpose. Now don't get me wrong, GOD does expect us to prepare ourselves mentally, physically and spiritually for opportunities, but He will also show us exactly how sovereign He is and He will use or advance someone that is the least likely in mans eyesight. All the planning and preparation we do may mean nothing if what we are planning and preparing for is not in GOD's plan for our lives. Zechariah 4:6 clearly states *"Not by might, nor by power, but by my spirit, saith the Lord of host."*

If you've read the Bible, I'm sure that you've come across some of the unlikely people that GOD has used throughout the scriptures. Rahab the harlot, stuttering Moses, the Christian killer Paul, David, who was so unlikely that Samuel was ready to anoint his older brother king because he looked the part, Samson, who was so unlikely that the people around him and even his wife had to ask him where his strength lied. These are just a few of the unlikely people that GOD has used throughout the Bible. Gideon is another, who may be lesser known than the others listed, who GOD chose to do extraordinary things through. Gideon's story shows us that it doesn't matter how small you think you are, how little education you have, how much in debt you are, or what society thinks of you, GOD can still do great things through you! It doesn't matter what man says, if GOD says you can do it…proceed with confidence!

No matter where you might be in your life at this present time or how bad you may be feeling about yourself, that has nothing to do with GOD's ability to do awesome things in you and through you! Please read the full story of Gideon in the book of Judges, if you haven't done so already. If that story doesn't convince you that GOD can greatly use unlikely people, let me remind you that if Jesus could use two fish and five loaves of bread to feed five thousand men (not including woman and children), how much more could GOD do through you with what you already have? The key to unlocking this is your belief. Jesus told twelve "unlikely" disciples in John 14:12 that *"he that believeth on me, the works that I do, he shall do also; and greater works than these shall he do..."*

Remember: The key to GOD using you effectively for His kingdom is your belief. Begin to believe that GOD can use an unlikely person, such as you and I, and see what begins to happen in your life!

Day 7

The Power of Prayer

Read: Amos 7: 2 & 3
"O Lord GOD, forgive, I pray! Oh, that Jacob may stand, for he is small!
So the Lord relented concerning this. "It shall not be," saith the Lord."

As we continue to deal with things that seemingly will not go away; financial difficulties, sickness, relationship problems, disobedient children, job stress etc, etc, it's important to remember that prayer does change things. I know that statement has become somewhat common these days, but for those of us who have gone through intense "stuff" and cried & prayed all night to GOD, we know for a fact that prayer does change things.

Many times we are totally unaware of how prayer changes things. We often are praying to GOD asking Him to change a particular situation, and He's not always going to do that. The situation itself doesn't present a problem for GOD; He can change that at anytime. What GOD often will do when we are praying about a situation is this, He begins to change us so that we are better able to deal with the situation.

The Bible says in Philipians 4: 6 & 7 that we should not worry about anything or any situation but concerning all things, though prayer and supplication, we are to make our request known to GOD. Then the peace of GOD, which surpasses all understanding, will guard our hearts and minds. That simply means that He is not changing the situation but He will give you such a level of peace in the midst of your circumstances that people will not be able to understand how you are handling things so well.

Amos shows us exactly what to do about, seemingly, impossible situations. His prayer, and GOD's response to it, reminds us how powerful prayer can be in the face of our troubles. I firmly believe that many of us have no idea what kind of changes we orchestrate or what kind of pain we spare others and ourselves when we simply fall down on our knees and pray.

Remember: A songwriter by the name of Joseph M. Scriven penned the words to a song in 1855 that truly expresses the point about prayer. In his song titled "What a Friend We Have in Jesus", Scriven wrote "Oh what peace we often forfeit. Oh, what needless pains we bear. All because we do not carry everything to GOD in prayer."

Day 8

You Are Blessed!

Read: I Peter 3:14 (NKJV)
"But even if ye suffer for righteousness' sake, you are blessed:"

There are many things that we go through in life, especially after we've come to Christ, which does not fit the worldly definition of being blessed. The world defines being blessed by the things their eyes can see; who has the biggest house, who has the most cars, who has the most "bling-bling". While GOD does bless us with these things, the Bible tells us that the things that are seen are temporal but it's the things that are not seen that are eternal (II Corinthians 4:18). And that is where I believe the real blessings can be found in a person's life. That's the message that Simon Peter used to encourage believers who were being persecuted by the Roman Empire in I & II Peter, and that's the message that I would like to share with all of you today. Although things may appear bad on the outside, you are indeed blessed!

People, if we let them, will try to convince us that GOD's blessings lie only in the abundance of things in our life. But the things and GOD's blessings are often two separate and distinct things. Genesis 26:12 says "Then Isaac sowed in that land, and received in the same year an hundred fold: and the Lord blessed him." It appears to me that the hundred-fold return and the blessings of the Lord are two separate things entirely. I'm sure that we've all heard stories of very wealthy people who have lived miserable lives because, although they had many things, they lacked the blessings of the Lord. Proverbs 15:16 tells us *"Better is little with the fear of the Lord than great treasure and trouble therewith."*

So where can the blessings of the Lord be found? I believe they can be found in the Fruits of the Spirit. When the Holy Spirit comes upon you and gives you love, joy, peace, longsuffering, gentleness, goodness, faith, meekness and temperance (Galatians 5: 22 & 23), that's when you know and realize that you are blessed. No matter what is happening on the outside, when you have the Fruits of the Spirit residing within you, you never lose sight of the fact that you are blessed. So although you may be dealing with some problems right now, remember that Paul reminds us in Acts 14:22 that we must "continue in faith, and that we must through much tribulation enter into the kingdom of GOD." That's where our real blessing can be found for all of the suffering that we have to endure.

Remember: *"Blessed are they which are persecuted for righteousness' sake: for theirs is the kingdom of heaven.*

Blessed are ye, when men shall revile you, and persecute you, and shall say all manner of evil against you falsely for my sake.

Rejoice, and be exceeding glad: for great is your reward in heaven" (Matthew 5: 10 – 12)

Day 9

It's All About Who You Know

Read: Daniel 11:32 (NKJV)
"but the people who know their GOD shall be strong, and carry out great exploits."

We live in a society that feels success often depends on who you know. A lot of people spend valuable time and money trying to position themselves to be in the company of the "right" people, whether that means going to the "right" school, living in the "right" neighborhood, or joining the "right" church or fraternity. This type of attitude frequently leads to disappointment as people realize that their success in not dependent on knowing the "right" people. Your success, and mine, is tied directly to us coming into the knowledge of GOD and knowing GOD is different from the way that we often say that we "know" people.

The dictionary defines "know" in several different ways. The ones that stand out to me are these; "to have a practical understanding or, as through experience" and "to discern the character or nature of". So to really know someone is to have a deep, intimate relationship with them to a point where you begin to understand their motives, their desires, how they feel about you and the things that you do that gives them pleasure or pain. Truly knowing someone is not just seeing them every now and then or spending maybe a few hours every year with them. No, to really know someone you've got to spend a great deal of time with him or her in various situations, both good and bad. The time we spend in thought, prayer, worship, and bible study is what GOD desires most of us and this is the only way we will ever get to the point of truly "knowing" Him.

The above scripture in Daniel states that the people who know their GOD shall be strong and carry out great exploits. I believe the type of strength Daniel is referring to is not necessarily physical strength but it's also the inner strength to handle all of the difficulties that life throws our way. There are some battles in life that can only be won using your inner strength. When things are going haywire on the job, in your home, or in your finances, no matter how physically strong you are, you can fall totally apart unless you have the inner strength that knowing GOD supplies. The 1st division of Psalms tells us that a blessed man's "delight is in the law of the Lord, and in His law doth he meditate day and night." (Psalms 1:2) This is the way that we come to the knowledge of GOD. Spend time in His word, think about it's truths throughout the day, ask GOD for wisdom and understanding for He gives it *"liberally and upbraideth not"* (James 1:5). Then, and only then, shall you be strong like a tree planted by the rivers of water, that brings forth fruit in it's season. Your leaves shall not wither and whatsoever you do shall prosper (Psalms 1:3). In other words, you shall do great exploits!

Remember: Knowing GOD is the key to your success!

Day 10

Shelter in the Time of Storm
Read: Joel 3:16 (NKJV)
"The heavens and the earth will shake: but the Lord will be a shelter for His people."

We are living in very stressful and uncertain times. The threat of terrorism, economic instability, and many other public and private events make this one, if not the most, uncertain time for all people worldwide. The thing that we must remember is that no matter what is going on in our lives, GOD is in control. And since He is in control, as the scripture in Joel 3:16 points out, He will shelter *His* people during these uncertain times.

It's important that we remember that GOD never promised us that we would not experience earth-shaking events in our lives. In fact the Bible says that "many are the afflictions of the righteous BUT the Lord delivers them from them all!" (Psalms 34:19). We are going to go through some very hard times & experiences. The key to enduring those times is directly related to whom we put our faith and trust in. GOD doesn't say in Joel 3:16 that He would stop the heavens and earth from shaking; He promises to simply be a shelter for His people while the heavens and earth are shaking around them.

Compare Joel 3:16 with the parable of the builder found in Matthew 7: 24 – 27 and I believe that you'll see why your ability to withstand storms is determined by whom you choose to put your faith and trust in. Joel 3:16 says that the heavens and earth will shake; Matthew 7:24 says that the *"rains descended, and the floods came, and the winds blew, and beat upon the house"*. Both are telling us that we are going to experience some serious times in our lives. Joel tells us that the Lord will be a shelter for His people during these times, His people being those that believe and trust in Him. Jesus tells us in Matthew 7 that, even though the storm came against the house, "it fell not because it was founded upon a rock". That rock, as we know, is the word of GOD.

This shelter in the time of storm is only guaranteed to those who build their house upon the rock of GOD's word. Knowing, believing and trusting in His word will allow you to endure the storms of life. I dare you to line up with GOD's word, begin putting your faith & trust in Him, and believe that *"all things work together for good to them that love GOD"* (Romans 8:28) and watch as He begins to shelter you from the effects of the storms in your life!

Remember: Many storms will come into your life but GOD stands ready to shelter you from each and every one of them.

Day 11

Handling the Corrections in Your Life

Read: Job 14: 7 –9

"For there is hope of a tree, if it be cut down, that it will sprout again, and that the tender branch thereof will not cease.
Though the root thereof wax old in the earth, and the stock thereof die in the ground;
Yet through the scent of water it will bud, and bring forth boughs like a plant."

There are times in our lives when things seem to be going more backwards than forwards. It feels as if everything is going horribly wrong in our lives, falling apart right in front of our eyes. Although all of us have or will go through times like this, it's important to remember that tough times won't last and GOD often will take you backwards to propel you to higher places. That may sound crazy to some of you but that's exactly what GOD allowed to happen to Job, and that is what frequently happens in the financial markets of today. In the stock market it's called a "market correction". For the benefit of those not familiar with the term, allow me to give some background on market corrections to illustrate how they apply to the above scripture and to our lives.

A correction can be described simply as a small, temporary drop in the price of stocks in a financial market. The term is often used to describe a decline in price after a period of rising prices. It's interesting to note that these corrections are considered beneficial for the long-term health of the markets. History shows us that new market highs are reached after every correction or "crash". Most of you will remember the stock market "crash" of 1987 and the many lives that were destroyed and even lost in the panic that followed. But, if you look at the numbers, you'll realize that if more people would have understood that it was a correction to make the markets more efficient and not lose their faith, they would be a lot better off now almost 20 years later. On October 19, 1987, the Dow Jones Industrial Average (DJIA) crashed from a high of 2,722.42, reached in August of that year, ending the day at 1,738 losing almost half of it's value in almost two months. While that is admittedly bad, look at where the average is today. As I write this, the DJIA begins the day at 10,213.22. That's an almost 600% increase in value from the end of day price on October 19, 1987! What's my point? It's simply this, we must realize that, like Job, we have to maintain our faith & hope as we go through the corrections in our lives. Job went through a horrific period in his life that some say lasted for only a few months. But because he was able to hold onto his faith and say things like *"though He slay me, yet will I trust Him"* (Job 13:15), GOD blessed him with twice as much as he had lost (Job 41:10). When you look at the history of the stock market, each time the market corrects itself (1929, 1987, 1990 for example), it rebounds from these lows to attain higher heights than it previously attained. Don't let the temporary bumps or hiccups in life tear you down. They're nothing more than corrections that GOD allows in your life to take you higher than you currently are. As Job said, if there is hope for a tree if it just gets the *scent* of water, after it's cut down and it's roots are old, to sprout and bring forth fruit then surly there is hope for you and I as we go through the corrections in our lives. It will be important for you to read, meditate on and keep close to your heart what Paul told the church at Corinth in II Corinthians 4:17 *"For our light afflictions, which are but for a moment, worketh for us a far more exceeding and eternal weight of glory;"*

Remember: the correction is needed in order for GOD to get you to the place that He's predestined for your life.

Day 12

GOD's Maturation Process

Read: II Corinthians 12:10
"Therefore I take pleasure in infirmities, in reproaches, in necessities, in persecutions, in distresses for Christ's sake:"

There is nothing like the stress we experience when we are going through things in our lives. Whether it's tough times at work, problems at home, financial difficulties or the stress that comes with feeling that everyone and everything is coming against you, dealing with these events is not pleasant at all. I will admit that I have never enjoyed the times in my life when I faced challenges and I was initially confused when I read Paul's words to the church at Corinth in II Corinthians 12:10. But after growing in wisdom, which GOD gives to all of us liberally, I can fully understand and appreciate Paul's words. As I've said previously, GOD uses the things that we go through to get us where He wants for us to be.

Looking back at my life, I can fully see how GOD used everything that I went through to develop me into the person that I am today. I realize that I could not have the testimony that I have now without having gone through the tests in my past. The hard times, the personal attacks, the struggles that I've faced, even the bad decisions that I made, I had to realize that GOD sent them or allowed them to make me better and to mature me to the level that He needed me to be in my life. I know that if you are going through a storm right now these words may be difficult to hear or accept, but believe me after you come out you will thank GOD that you went through all that you did. You have to constantly remind yourself that you serve a GOD of better things. Hebrews 11:40 begins by telling us that *"GOD having provided some better thing for us...",* which literally means that GOD would not take us through all the things that we go through to give us something worse than what we had. That is why I, like Paul, can truly delight when I am going through tough times because I know that there is something better waiting for me on the other side of my problems.

If you're going through a tough situation right now I would like to encourage you to remain steadfast, unmovable and faithful, understanding that GOD often uses seemingly bad times in our lives to mature us and to strengthen our inner man. Your challenges are all a part of your maturation process. If you still can't fully understand this, take a look at the life of Joseph and all that he had to go through to get where

GOD predestined him to be. Although GOD showed him early on where he would end up in life, Joseph had to go through the pit, being sold into slavery, being lied on in Potipher's house and, finally, going to jail to ensure that he was fully matured to handle all that GOD had planned for his life.

Remember: although things may be painful at the present time, it's all a part of the process.

Day 13

Speaking What You Believe

Read: Joel 3:10 (b)
"...let the weak say, I am strong."

Too often, we let the everyday ups and downs of life get us to the point of saying some very negative things. Contrary to what the word of GOD says, we tend to say things like "I'll never get out of this debt" or "this is all that I'll ever be in life". The scriptures clearly state that we are often snared by the words of our mouths (Proverbs 12:13). Since snared means trapped, when we say these negative things, we are actually speaking them into existence in our lives, thus trapping ourselves in a situation that GOD clearly did not intend for us to be in. Proverbs 18:21 says that **"Death and life are in the power of the tongue."** Keep on telling yourself that you'll never be more than you are or that you'll never get out of your existing situation, and that's exactly what will happen. You'll never do more or be more because you've trapped yourself mentally with the words that you've spoken. One of the very first steps you must take in your journey to transform your life is to stop planting negative seeds of doubt into your own head, continually telling yourself what you can't do. Begin by saying, and believing, that "I can do all things through Christ who strengthens me!"

When we are faced with a tough task or seemingly insurmountable odds, that's when we must allow our faith to shine the brightest. Hebrews 11:1 tells us that *"Faith is the substance of things hoped for; the evidence of things not seen"* and I believe that it is through our faith that we begin to call those things that are not as though they were (Romans 4:17). If you believe that you're coming out of debt, start saying it! If you believe that GOD is going to bring you to a higher level of prosperity, start speaking it! Silent faith will move no mountains. Jesus said that the only way to move a mountain is to speak to it! You have to not only believe in your heart that things will change, you've got to also confess it with your mouth. Romans 10:9 tells us that's the way in which we are saved and I believe that's the only way that things begin to change in our lives.

As you continue this journey, it will be important for you to apply the words that GOD gave the prophet Joel in the above scripture. Yes, you may be going through a difficult time in your life, and yes, you may have even made some mistakes in your life that you think you'll never overcome. All that means absolutely nothing to GOD! It's because of Him that we, the weak, can say that we are strong (II Corinthians 12: 9 & 10). It's all up to you. You've got to know that things will never change for you if you don't begin speaking positive things into existence in your life. Have the faith to say that your more than a conqueror, your suppose to be the head and not the tail, above and not beneath and see how GOD begins to do exceeding abundantly above all that you could ever ask or think. And it will all be according to the power that is already inside of you. You just have to speak it!

Remember: The things that you say will eventually come to pass in your life.

Day 14

Awaiting Your Due Date

Read: I Peter 5:6
"Humble yourselves therefore under the mighty hand of GOD, that He may exalt you in due time:"

One of the toughest positions to be in is to know that you have something inside of you but not being in the right situation to show others around you all that you can do. Many of you know that you have the ability to be great leaders, to do extraordinary things or even know that you've been called into the ministry. But any good thing attempted or done at the wrong time often results in failure and defeat. This is why Simon Peter instructs us in the above scripture that we should put away our pride and allow GOD to exalt us in due time.

Patience is an essential element of humility, as well as an integral part of transforming your life. Humility shows itself in submission; it's the ability to put away our own agenda for GOD's agenda, even if His agenda is not the same or on a different timeframe than ours. GOD may have given you the abilities to do great things but just because you have the abilities does not mean that now is the right time for you to showcase those abilities. They're not DUE yet! It's like when a woman is pregnant. She knows within a few weeks (or days) after conception that she has a baby developing inside of her. But it would be disastrous if that baby were delivered too soon before its due date. Over a nine month period, there is needed development & maturation that's going on inside the woman so that when her due date arrives she will deliver a healthy baby.

The same holds true for you. You have to remember that you must not only be called and have the talent to do something, you must wait to be sent into your calling in GOD's due time, not yours. I know that it's hard but that's the only way that GOD will truly get the glory that He desires. Humility is essential to our relationship with GOD. If we want to walk in GOD's grace (His unmerited favor), we must lay aside our pride (and our need to be seen), and be humble. Our pride demands that GOD bless us in light of our merits (real or imagined) but GOD blesses us according to HIS grace. That's why Psalms 16:18 warns us that "Pride goes before a destruction and a haughty (arrogant or exalted) spirit comes before a fall." (NKJV)

Remember: You may be called but you must wait to be sent. If you are in a humbling situation right now, remain humble and submit to GOD's plan. He knows the "due date" when you are to be exalted. Keep growing, maturing and developing so that you're fully prepared when your due date arrives.

Day 15

Strengthen Your Inner Man

Read: Ephesians 3: 14 – 16
"For this cause I bow my knees unto the Father of our Lord Jesus Christ, of whom the whole family in heaven and earth is named.
That He would grant you, according to the riches of His glory, to be strengthened with might by His spirit in the inner man;"

When I read the above scripture, I immediately begin to think of an attribute that many people have but few recognize, and that is "intestinal fortitude". It really comes together when you look up the word fortitude; Webster's defines it as **"strength of mind that allows one to endure pain or adversity with courage."** So, from that definition, and the above scripture, I've come to the conclusion that it is not outer strength that causes people to be victorious in life. It is inner strength that allows us to prevail. I can testify that life will send tests against you that cannot be won through outer strength. Unfortunately, most people don't recognize their own strength because they are looking for strength that can be seen. As an example, Delilah would not have had to ask Samson where his strength lied if she could see it with her eyes (Judges

16:6). He looked normal on the outside but he had incredible inner strength!

It's important to note that inner strength is more than will power. Inner strength doesn't come from our will but it comes from the will of GOD. It comes from being tied into GOD's will and purpose for our lives. The secret to Paul's success in life was in who he was tied to. He sounded like a braggart but he knew that he could do absolutely ANYTHING, not because he was so great, but because he knew who he was tied into (I can do all things through Christ who strengthens me). What he's saying is "the reason I can is because I have inner strength!"

The riches of GOD's glory is that you'd be strengthened in your inner man. Stop wrestling with outer things. Too often we talk to an eternal GOD about temporal problems that will mean little in a few years. GOD wants to strengthen who we really are, not who we appear to be.

The whole fight with the enemy is not for the external but for the internal. The devil is trying to break your inner strength using outer things to control your mind. The more outer things effect you, the more successful the enemy is over you. So, how do you win this battle and begin to transform your life? Simply by facing outer peril with inner strength. Begin by building up your intestinal fortitude!

Remember: Inner strength will lead to outer success!

Day 16

Pursue It with Confidence

Read: Hebrews 10: 35 & 36
"Cast not away therefore your confidence, which hath great recompense of reward.
For ye have need of patience, that, after ye have done the will of GOD, ye might receive the promise."

If GOD has given you a vision, remain confident no matter what comes your way. Never allow fear, doubt or what others might say is impossible to creep in and keep you from doing what GOD has for you to do. As the Hebrews 10:35 tells us, don't throw away your trust in the Lord, regardless of what happens. Just keep in mind the great reward that it brings!

To do the will of GOD is to follow His instructions. Whether He gave you specific directions or spiritual references, do exactly what He told you to do. When things aren't happening fast enough, we have a tendency to try and jump into the driver's seat and attempt to make things happen a lot sooner than GOD has planned. Remember this one thing, although He has given you the vision, GOD is in control; you're just along for the ride. If He's given you His promise, hold on to it, what GOD has for you is for you!

Habakkuk 2:3 says it a lot better that I can:
"For the vision is yet for an appointed time, but at the end it shall speak, and not lie: though it tarry, wait for it; because it will surely come."
If there is only one thing that you take away from this book, I hope that it would be this: there is a big difference in **thinking** that you can do the impossible and **believing** that you can do the impossible. God has given us His word and we are not only to think that His word is true
but we must also believe that His word is true. For if you believe *"...nothing shall be impossible to you"* (Matthew 17:20).

Remember: The only way you win is if you keep on fighting! Regardless of how things look on the outside, continue to persevere and pursue your dreams.

Day 17

It Simply Won't Compare

Read: Romans 8:18 & 19
"For I reckon that the sufferings of this present time are not worthy to be compared with the glory which shall be revealed in us.
For the earnest expectation of the creature waiteth for the manifestation of the sons of God."

Romans 8:18 & 19 is a scripture that should be remembered by every person that has ever picked up a Bible. The scripture is telling us that no matter how terrible your situation may seem right now, it doesn't compare to what GOD will reveal to us in this life and in eternity. Put another way, whatever you have to go through in SEED form doesn't compare to the HARVEST that GOD has in store for you!

I didn't grow up on a farm but if I understand what I've heard, when farmers are plowing a field, no matter what impediment they face in the process, they must keep on plowing. Their plow hits a rock, what do they do? Move the rock and keep on plowing. They run into a root, what do they do? Dig up the root and keep on plowing. They're doing this because they know that no matter what obstacles they face during the process of plowing, they simply do not compare in any way to the harvest that they will experience when the seeds that were planted come to fruition.

Verse 19 should excite and motivate all of us. For it is telling us that GOD is just waiting for us to walk into the promises that He has spoken over our lives! If He promised it to you, He will bring it to pass in your life. GOD is not a liar nor is He an "Indian-giver". Romans 11:29 tells us that *the gifts and calling of GOD are without repentance.* The New King James Version really brings out the point in this scripture; it replaces repentance with "irrevocable". So once again we see that if GOD started it, He's gonna finish it!

Remember: What you're going through just doesn't compare to the blessings that are on the other side of your problems!

Day 18

You're Bigger Than That

Read: I John 4: 3 & 4

"And the spirit that confesseth not that Jesus Christ is come in the flesh is not of GOD: and this is that spirit of antichrist, whereof ye have heard that it should come; and even now already is in the world. Ye are of GOD, little children, and have overcome them: because greater is He that is in you, than he that is in the world."

Although GOD told us that there are going to be many things that we must suffer for His name's sake (Acts 9:16), He never told us that we would be defeated by these attacks. Every trial and tribulation that we go through is meant to develop us and if we are attentive to GOD, He can reveal His ultimate purpose to us. Remember that GOD's purpose is bigger than any of the day-to-day problems that the world will throw our way. And, as the scripture above tells us, we've overcome the world and any of the problems that come with it because of WHO resides within us. I Corinthians 3:16 asks us this question, *"Know ye not that ye are the temple of GOD and that the spirit of GOD dwelleth in you?"* If your body has the spirit of GOD residing in it, then

73

you have to believe that you are truly bigger than anything that life can throw your way!

You must begin to believe, wholeheartedly, that you are bigger than any of the problems that you may currently face in your life. You have to be able to say, with confidence, that all things will work together for good because you love the Lord! Begin to believe in your heart that you are suppose to be the *"head and not the tail, above and not beneath"*. You can begin to make these claims now, regardless of how things look in your life, because the word says that you are guaranteed victory over all the situations in your life.

Remember: Life cannot throw anything at you that GOD hasn't given you the victory over!

Blessed in a Mess

Read: Matthew 13: 24 – 30
"Let both grow together until harvest: and in the time of harvest I will say to the reapers, Gather ye together first the tares, and bind them in bundles to burn them: but gather the wheat into my barn."
(Verse 30)

I think that it's safe to say that every person reading this has, is or will soon be going through problems in your life that seem utterly ridiculous. Most of these things are situations that, although they are tough to deal with at the time, have little or no bearing on our destiny. They are outer attacks that the devil sends to effect your mind. II Corinthians 10:4 & 5 tells us *"For the weapons of our warfare are not carnal, but mighty through GOD to the pulling down of strongholds; casting down imaginations, and every high thing that exalts itself against the knowledge of GOD, and bringing into captivity every thought to the obedience of Christ."* You have to understand that the riches of GOD's glory is that you are strengthened in your inner man (Ephesians 3:16) so that you are able to effectively handle these outer attacks that come against your mind. I beg of you, if you want to

75

experience a transformed life, to stop wresting with outer things.

GOD sends His word to us according to His purpose, so it may not respond to your problem. The only way the word will respond to your problem is if your problem threatens GOD's purpose for your life. It's interesting to note in the parable that the enemy's purpose in sowing the tares was to not only destroy the wheat, but he sowed the tares to also get the workers thinking more about the tares than the wheat. But the wise farmer (GOD) will not allow the enemy to succeed. For He knows that the tares cannot destroy what He has already done!

Another important key to experiencing a transformed life is to learn how to be blessed in a mess. Sometimes we ask GOD why is it that He will not fix our mess, and His answer is that the mess has nothing to do with His purpose. If the devil can keep your mind focused on the problems in your life, he's won the battle. You've got to come to the point of realizing that if the enemy is attacking you in a way that is not threatening to your destiny, it's not worth your attention. After you've lived a while, you'll come to realize that a whole lot of stuff that you're worrying about now, really doesn't matter in the end.

Remember: If GOD says that He is going to bless you, pay no attention to what's happening around you even when those things seem contrary to GOD's promise. What He said WILL come to pass!

Day 20

A Change is All You Need

Read: Matthew 9: 16 – 17
"No man putteth a piece of cloth unto an old garment, for that which is put in to fill it up taketh from the garment, and the rent is made worse. Neither do men put new wine into old bottles: else the bottles break, and the wine runneth out, and the bottles perish: but they put new wine into new bottles, and both are preserved."

We sometimes talk to other people, believers and non-believers, about the frustrations in life that we are experiencing. It sometimes seems that we are not able to come into the blessing and promises of GOD, and we are looking for someone to supply an answer to a question that only GOD's word can supply an answer to. When seeking answers to the questions regarding the promises of GOD, it's important to remember that the answers can be found more in what WE are not doing as opposed to what GOD is not doing. Unless you truly change as the above scriptures suggest (old things are passed away, behold I will do a new thing), you will continue to experience some of the same frustrations that you've always faced and still not understand why.

Too often, we expect to receive different results without changing the way that we are currently doing things. That is just plain backwards. You can't continue to pray and ask GOD to bless you financially but continue to be an unfaithful steward over what you currently have, blowing all of your pay without thinking about GOD or your future. You can't continue to ask GOD to bless you with a meaningful relationship yet continue to exhibit anti-social behaviors which no one in their right mind would want to spend any time around. You can't continue to ask GOD to bless you with a more fulfilling job, yet you can't consistently get to work on time and you're not performing at an acceptable level on the job you already have. I am writing this not to attack nor condemn anyone. I'm writing this because I know these things to be true from my personal experiences. There has to be a change before GOD releases His blessing because, if not, the blessing will fail to be a blessing.

The scripture is very clear in stating that GOD will not pour new blessings into old methodologies! There has to be a change in the way that you do things BEFORE GOD opens up the windows of heaven. To change is the basic definition of "transform". So to truly transform your life you will have to recognize the things that must be changed in your life. The sooner this is done, the sooner GOD will begin to release the blessings that He has spoken over your life!

Remember: You have to change your methods in order to receive GOD's blessings!

Day 21

The Value in Being Patient

Read: James 1: 2 – 4
"My brethren, count it all joy when ye fall into divers temptations;
Knowing this, that the trying of your faith worketh patience.
But let patience have her perfect work, that ye may be perfect and entire, wanting nothing."

Although it's one of the hardest things for most of us to master, patience is a necessity as you begin the process of transforming your life. It's tough but we have to remember that GOD desires to bless us but we may have some maturing to do or lessons or learn before He can release certain blessings in our life. As James wrote in the above scripture, we have a settled peace (JOY) in the midst of our trials, which allows patience to finish its perfect work so that we can become complete, not lacking anything. We can have this level of peace during our trials because we know that whatever we are going through is in GOD's permissive will.

A man whom we can learn much from when it comes to the value of being patient is Joseph. Through his experiences (GOD given dream, to the pit, to slavery, to Potipher's house, to prison, and finally to ruler over all of Egypt), we learn four important lessons regarding patience:

1) **Learning to wait strengthens our confidence in GOD:** People who are forced to live in circumstances that are totally beyond their control, emerge from them knowing more than ever before that without GOD they can do nothing! Their faith, though refined by fire, comes forth like gold. At Mind the same time, their self-confidence develops but is focused in Jesus Christ. Look at what Paul says in Galatians 2:20 *"I am crucified with Christ: nevertheless I live; yet not I, but Christ liveth in me: and the life which I now live in the flesh I live by the faith of the Son of GOD, who loved me, and gave himself for me."*

2) **A period of waiting often allows time for us to develop:** There are lessons that cannot be learned apart from going through a period of waiting, and often that period is in the context of adversity. In the midst of your adversities, you will often grow closer to GOD. And although you may sometimes waver and regress, you will bounce back more determined to reflect GOD's character in your life.
   Transforming Your Life by Renewing Your Mind

3) **A period of waiting often creates opportunities for advancement that may not happen otherwise:** Joseph's life teaches us that GOD's timing is perfect! Our temptation is to get in a hurry when things are not going the way we think they should. Perhaps GOD is trying to say to us during our impatient times "Wait, and if you do, what I have for you will be far greater than anything you can create on your own." This, of course, is not an excuse for inactivity & laziness. For we all know that faith, without works, is dead.

4) **A period of waiting through difficulty and pain helps us develop wisdom we otherwise might not receive:** If we can see how being patient, even through tough times, is actually an opportunity for growth, it can enable us to develop wisdom and judgement far beyond our years.

Remember: Ecclesiates 7:8 *"Better is the end of a thing than the beginning thereof: and the patient in spirit is better than the proud in spirit"*

Day 22

Get There…By Any Means Necessary!

Read: Mark 2: 4 – 5
"And when they could not come nigh unto him for the press, they uncovered the roof where He was: and when they had broken it up, they let down the bed wherein the sick of palsy lay.
When Jesus saw their faith, He said unto the sick of palsy, Son, thy sins be forgiven thee."

The road to Christ, and to your goals/dreams, will not be easy. Since we know before hand that the road will not be easy, if we want to get to Christ and attain success, we have to have the mindset that we will do whatever is necessary to get to Him and to "it". In the scripture, we see four men who collected their paralyzed friend and attempted to take him to Jesus to be healed. Because of the large crowd that had gathered, they could not reach Jesus by conventional methods. Did they allow that to stop them? Absolutely not! These men cut a hole in the roof and used a rope to lower their paralyzed friend down into the presence of Jesus. When Jesus saw the faith the man had in doing whatever he needed to do to come into His presence, He immediately blessed him.

On your road to Christ and success, you should not let obstacles stop your progress. Even though you'll encounter some rough times and things will not be as easy as you'd hoped for, be like this paralyzed man and his friends. Do whatever you need to do to get where you want to be! Some people will look at you and think that you're crazy for going through all the trouble to get into the presence of Christ. But remember that fulfilling a dream often does not come easy or within the realm of the conventional. If you really want something bad enough, you'll do whatever you need to do to get it. That includes climbing up the side of a house, cutting a hole in the roof and lowering yourself on a rope!

Even though men will criticize you and say all manner of evil against you when you begin to do the unconventional, don't let that stop you. GOD will truly bless you when He sees that you are willing to do the seemingly impossible and unorthodox to get to Him and obtain the promises that He has spoken over your life.

Remember: GOD expects you to get to Him and experience all that He has planned for your life by any means necessary!

Day 23

Get Up!

Read: Joshua 7:10
"And the Lord said unto Joshua, Get thee up; wherefore liest thou thus upon thy face?"

Although He does realize that our life will be hard and full of many challenging experiences, GOD does not expect us to wallow in self-pity after we've experienced setbacks in our life. Setbacks and trials are both a part of our walk as Christians. In fact, Paul tells us in Acts 14:22 that *"we through much tribulation enter into the kingdom of GOD"*. GOD does not want, nor expects, us to go through things in our lives that may not work out as we had planned, and lose hope. That's not faith! Our faith is proven by how well we go through things because we don't need faith after we gain our victories; we need faith when it doesn't look like we'll be victorious at all.

When we experience defeat in our lives, GOD expects us to regroup and reevaluate the situation. He never intended for you to be defeated, but He will allow you to experience defeat if you are not fully aligned with what He's instructed you to do. That was GOD's expectation of Joshua in the 7th chapter. Like

Joshua, it's important that you evaluate the reason, the *real* reason, things are happening in your life. Looking at Joshua's defeat at Ai, we can see that the real reason for the children of Israel's defeat was sin. If you read the entire 7th chapter, you'll realize that GOD did not fail to keep His promise to Israel, Israel failed to keep its promise to GOD. Although it was the sin of only one man, Achan, GOD judged the entire city. I Corinthians 5:6 asks us *"Do you not know that a little leaven leavens the whole lump?"*

So Joshua experienced defeat not because of a problem he had with GOD. He experienced defeat because of a single problem in his camp. And the same could be true of you. Now the question is, what do you do when you're defeated and you realize that the problem is within? You do exactly what GOD instructed Joshua to do…GET UP! You must realize that GOD's purpose is for us to live a life of unbroken victory but He will allow us to experience defeat if we are not in obedience to His word. Follow the instructions that GOD gave to Joshua in the 13th – 15th verses of the 7th chapter; go back and honestly reevaluate the situation and make the necessary changes to get back into alignment with GOD's word. You may realize that you have to let go of some friends, habits or "vices" that are hindering you from your blessings. But you have to be willing to give up in order to go up!

Remember: It doesn't matter whether you fall down or not. What matters most is how fast you get up after you fall!

Day 24

Your Blessing is on the "Right Side"

Read: John 21: 5- 6
"Then Jesus saith unto them, Children, have ye any meat? They answered him, No.
And He said unto them, Cast the net on the right side of the ship, and ye shall find. They cast therefore, and now they were not able to draw it for the multitude of fishes."

Often we wonder why are the things that GOD has spoken over our lives taking so long to come to fruition. Quite frankly, I believe, we are in the right place to receive our blessing but we are focused on the wrong things or positioned in the wrong direction. When you're focused on the wrong thing or positioned in the wrong direction, you will miss things or opportunities that are basically right in front of you. Another key to transforming your life then would be that you should begin to turn your attention to the "right" side.

Like the disciples in John 21:5, when you're unsuccessful at a task, you don't generally welcome questions about your progress. The scripture says that when the Lord asked them if they have any meat, they simply said "No". They didn't make any excuses but if the disciples were like some of us, considering that they had been fishing all night without catching one fish, this "No" answer was given with a bit of an attitude. They were in the right place to receive their blessing, they were just focused in the wrong direction. The difference really is not between simply facing to the right or the left. The difference for you as you begin to transform your life is between working with or without Divine guidance.

Think about this for a moment, all of you who are reading this, who have been tolling, working, wondering when "its" going to happen; success, or a blessing, for these disciples was only a boat's width away. Four, maybe six, feet from one side of the boat to the other – that's how close they were to success and they didn't even realize it! And you too might very well be "four to six feet" away from your biggest success in life. How do you move into position to receive your blessing? Simply by obeying the word of GOD. Deuteronomy 28:1 begins by telling us that *"It shall come to pass, if thou shalt harken diligently unto the voice of the Lord thy GOD..."* If you want GOD to release your blessing, begin to diligently obey His voice and all that He has instructed you to do. It's just that simple.

Perhaps GOD has been dealing with you, even speaking to you, but you thought His direction wasn't related to the challenge you face or the endeavor you've undertaken. The disciples could have said "We've been fishing all night. We're experts at this. What does moving four feet have to do with anything?" But when they did what Jesus told them to do, they were immediately on the "right side". So it may be with you. You might be very close to success in every sense of the word. All you have to do is decide to obey what GOD has instructed you to do. It's not magical or mystical. It's not even difficult; it's just a matter of doing what GOD has placed in your heart and mind to do. Step on the water, Peter, and do what others say is impossible!

Remember: Listening and obedience will unlock the blessings of GOD!

Day 25

Don't Lose Hope!

Read: Romans 15:13
"Now the GOD of hope fill you with all joy and peace in believing, that ye may abound in hope, through the power of the Holy Ghost."

No man or woman who has lost hope has ever been used by GOD to build up His kingdom. A person who has lost hope is not very useful to anyone for that matter. Their mind is so focused only on the things that they can see that they never allow their faith to shine through the clouds of life. The only way that some people were able to handle the vicissitudes of life was to keep their hope of better days intact. Look at the lives of Joseph, Noah, Moses, David & Paul. Imagine how different their lives would have turned out had they lost hope and gave up.

As you continue on your journey to transforming your life, it is of vital importance that you maintain your hope. And it's important to remember that it's the work of the Holy Spirit to impart hope (Romans 15:13). A person who is filled with the Holy Ghost will always be hopeful. Regardless of what's going on around them, they will be looking out into the future knowing that everything will be alright. They know this because they know that we serve a GOD of better things (Hebrews 11:40) and they know that all things will work together for their good (Romans 8:28). They also know that the GOD of all grace stands ready to do the impossible in their lives. There are some people who can testify that it was only by the grace and power of GOD that they were delivered out of seemingly hopeless situations. And if GOD can do that for them, He stands ready to do it for you also.

To maintain your hope, it's very important that you not let negative people cloud your inner circle. There's nothing like being around or constantly talking to people who are filled with hope. They tend to have a totally different way of looking at everything in life. They may be right in the middle of a hellish situation but they've been so transformed by the renewing of their minds that their focus is on the power of GOD and His ability to change situations. Hopeless people constantly throw a gloomy cloud over everything, looking at the dark side of things and always talking about the difficulties that are in the way. Basically, they have carnal minds and the word says that type of mindset is an "enmity against GOD" (Romans 8:7). A good working definition of enmity is "the state of opposition; hostility"; so basically a carnal mind doesn't like GOD and GOD doesn't like a carnal mind.

Regardless of how bad your situation is, don't lose hope. You can stand to lose everything else but you must fight to keep your hope. If you can find anyone that GOD has delivered from addictions, bankruptcy, divorce, financial bondage or anything else, you have to believe that He can deliver you as well, so why should you give up hope? A person who has lost hope is out of communion with GOD. He/she does not have the spirit of GOD controlling their thoughts. It's important to remember that the enemy tries to control our reality through illusions (II Corinthians 10:5), trying to make us believe that there is no hope for our situation. My prayer is that GOD will give you hope through the Holy Spirit, that you may be ever hopeful and that you may have the power that comes with the Holy Spirit (Act 1:8).

Remember: *"Faith is the substance of things hoped for, the evidence of things not seen"* (Hebrews 11:1) Exercise your faith by maintaining your hope!

Day 26

Don't Worry; GOD is on Your Side!

Read: Psalms 2:1 – 2
"Why do the heathen rage, and the people imagine a vain thing?
The kings of the earth set themselves, and the rulers take counsel together, against the LORD, and against His anointed,"

Like David in Psalms 2, many of us have asked why GOD allows His people, or His "anointed" ones, to suffer so greatly. Many of us have asked questions such as "GOD, why do you let certain things happen to me? Why do you allow people to treat me the way that they do?" You would think that GOD would stop the attacks and persecution but the truth is that GOD allows, and often sends troubles your way. Why? Because you're anointed and it's the things that you have to go through that pull the anointing out of you. To be anointed simply means to be empowered. So you wouldn't know how anointed, or empowered, you are until you've gone through some things in life.

It is, without exception, absolutely necessary for GOD's anointed to suffer. The moment you begin to accept and understand this, you will begin to rejoice in tribulation. You have to remember that while you do have victory in Christ Jesus (I Corinthians 15:57), there can be no victory without a battle. The same GOD who has promised to supply all of our needs according to His riches in glory, has also promised us that we will go through trials and tribulations in our lives. The trials and tribulations do have a divine purpose though and that is to bring death to the flesh. GOD is trying to get you to realize that you will not be able to handle the many trials and tribulations that will come in your life unless you fully abide and trust in Him, not your flesh. That is the only way to ensure victory.

When your enemies are mounting strong attacks against you and the devil thinks that he has torn down your faith with troubles, know that GOD is somewhere smiling on the situation. He's smiling because He knows that He will not allow you to go through, or be subjected to, anything beyond your anointing. I Corinthians 10:13 promises us that GOD *"will not suffer you to be tempted above that ye are able"*.

You're going through it because you're anointed (empowered) to handle it! So keep the faith during your trials and temptations. GOD is allowing them or sending them to pull something out of you and your having to go through it is proof positive that you're anointed (empowered) to have the victory over it!

Remember: If you're going through anything it's simply because GOD has given you the power to have victory over it, as long as you stay connected to Him!

Day 27

The Master of the One-Punch Knockout

Read: Genesis 41: 14 & 41
"Then Pharaoh sent and called Joseph, and they brought him hastily out of the dungeon: and he shaved himself, and changed his raiment, and came in unto Pharaoh.

And Pharaoh said unto Joseph, See, I have set thee over all the land of Egypt."

If you are a fan of boxing I think that you'll agree that the most exciting probability in the sport is that someone will get knocked out with a single punch. Many fighters have been ahead on the judges scorecards for the entire fight, only to get caught by a single punch that turns what was thought to be an easy victory seconds earlier, into a stunning defeat. These punches seem to come out of nowhere and turn things around so quickly that the people who witness the fight can't believe that the tide changed so quickly. These "miracles" happen in the boxing ring and they can happen in your life as well. We serve a GOD who is THE master of the one-punch knockout and the events in Joseph's life proves just that.

The life of Joseph can teach us many lessons. One of the most important and inspirational lessons, as you journey towards renewing your mind about situations, is that no matter how bad things may seem, GOD can change your situation around in seconds. Joseph woke up one morning a prisoner and by the end of that same day, Pharaoh had set him in change over all the land of Egypt. Only Pharaoh was to be greater in Egypt than Joseph (verse 40). If that isn't a one-punch knockout I don't know what is! For 17 years Joseph went through a beating that most of us could not stand. His life is proof that just because you lost a round or two doesn't mean that you won't win the fight. Joseph stayed faithful despite all that was happening to him and with one punch, GOD changed his entire life.

You may have had many things go wrong for you recently but in an instant, GOD can change your situation with one punch. Just when things are seemingly at there worst, and you're experiencing a beating that no one thinks you'll ever survive, that's when GOD can, and will, step in to deliver you. In II Corinthians 12:9, GOD tells Paul that *"my strength is made perfect in weakness"*. When things seem at their worst, that's when GOD steps in with His almighty power. With one punch He can change the rest of your life!

Remember: The only way you win is if you keep on fighting! You can't tell who will win the fight by looking at who won the last round! KEEP ON FIGHTING!

Day 28

Coming to Your Senses

Read: Luke 15:17
"And when he came to himself, he said, How many hired servants of my father's have bread enough to spare, and I perish with hunger?"

GOD has blessing set aside for us that we can't even imagine. Just as He promised the children of Israel that He would give them houses that they did not build and vineyards that they did not grow, He has promised us in His word that He would bless us exceeding abundantly above all that we could ask or think (Ephesians 3:20). Yet why is it that so many of us are living in conditions that are well below where GOD desires to take us? I believe that disobedience is at the heart and the only way to experience the levels of blessing that GOD has for you is to come to your senses and fully realize how much GOD desires to bless you.

Far too many of us are suffering and going through needless storms simply because we are not being obedient to the word of GOD. While disobedience may not have been at the heart of the prodigal son's problem in the above scripture, it wasn't until he

111

"came to himself" and realized that he was going through needless troubles and that his father could supply all of his needs, that his situation began to change. And the same is true for many of us. Some of us have not yet come to our senses and realized that we truly serve a GOD of better things who desires the best for us. The best will only come, your situation will only change, and you will be transformed, when you come to your senses and begin to fully obey the word of GOD.

Deuteronomy 28:1 tells us that *"it shall come to pass, if thou shalt hearken diligently unto the voice of the Lord thy GOD, to observe and to do all His commandments which I command thee this day, that the Lord thy GOD will set thee on high above all the nations of the earth."* This happens to be one of my favorite scriptures in all the Bible because it gives specific instructions on what it takes to go from the hog pen to the palace, from wandering to walking, from survival to success. If you would simply come to your senses and begin to hearken diligently unto the voice of the Lord and observe and do all He commands, He promises to take you from where you are and set you on a high place. Come to your senses and return unto your Father who has bread enough to spare, as you sit there starving living in a situation that GOD never intended for you to be in.

Remember: Coming to your senses is of utmost importance in transforming your life and renewing your mind.

Day 29

Bringing Things Back Together

Read: Deuteronomy 30: 2 –4
"And shalt return unto the Lord thy GOD, and shalt obey His voice according to all that I command thee this day, thou and thy children, with all thine heart, and with all thy soul;
That then the Lord thy GOD will turn thy captivity, and have compassion upon thee, and will return and gather thee from all the nations, whither the Lord thy GOD hath scattered thee.
If any of thine be driven out unto the outmost parts of the heaven, from thence will the Lord the GOD gather thee, and from thence will He fetch thee:"

All of us have, or will go through "scattering" events in our lives. Though they might be painful and tough to deal with, it's important that you know that it is not GOD's intention to leave your life in a scattered state. There are some events in life that we have no control over that will scatter or dismember us for a moment. But there are also many things that we willfully do that cause us to end up in a scattered state. These are the type of things that Moses was speaking about to the children of Israel in the above scripture and I believe that this is equally important today as we begin the journey to a transformed mind. Regardless of how broken up things may look right now in your life, GOD has the power to bring back together all of the broken pieces of your life!

As we all know, the children of Israel were delivered out of bondage and while on their way to the Promised Land, went through some scattering events because of their disobedience. Their disobedience and lack of faith caused them to stay in that scattered state for 40 years. Unfortunately, these are the same reasons that continue to keep some of us from realizing the promises that GOD has spoken over our lives. GOD has given us clear instructions throughout the Bible that will guarantee success and keep our lives together, yet we continue to try and do things our way. Amazingly, we still can't figure out why we can't keep things together, even though the word makes it painfully clear why. As an example, Psalms 1 gives us very clear instructions on what it takes to be blessed, but too many of us simply pay no attention to it's truths. It begins by stating this: *"Blessed is the man that walketh not in the counsel of the ungodly; nor standeth in the way of sinners, nor sitteth in the seat of the scornful"* While the word plainly states this, how many of you can admit to having gone through a scattered state, or are going through one right now, simply because of who you are associating with or are connected to?

The key to bringing the scattered pieces of your life back together lies in your ability to be obedient to what GOD has instructed us to do in His word. One of the reasons that I love GOD so much is that no matter how much I have messed up in my past, if I turn from those ways and ask for forgiveness, GOD stands ready to shower His mercy upon my life. Deuteronomy 30:3 says that *"**GOD will turn thy captivity, and have compassion upon thee**"* if you simply return to Him and begin to obey His word. No matter how far gone you think you are, how bad things might be, or no matter where you are right now, the word says in verse 4 that GOD can, and will *"fetch"* you and begin to bring back all the scattered pieces of your life.

Remember: No matter where you are, you're never out of GOD's reach! He stands ready to deliver you from where you are, to where He intends for you to be.

Day 30

The Deliverer!

Read: II Timothy 3: 11 & 12
"...what persecutions I endured: but out of them all the Lord delivered me.
Yea, and all that will live godly in Christ Jesus shall suffer persecution"

As I've mentioned in various sections of this devotional, although it may be difficult to handle while we are going through it, it's the persecutions or tough times that we have to endure that actually strengthens us to become all that GOD has called us to be. Without persecutions/challenges in our lives we would never reach the point where we totally put our faith and trust in GOD. If we have never been sick, we would never know that GOD was a healer. If we have never been broke or without, we would never know that GOD was a provider. If we have never been discomforted, we would never know that GOD was a comforter. It is very important that you remember the two things that Paul wrote to Timothy in the above scriptures that will help you mightily as you go through the process of transforming your life: (1) if you put your trust in GOD, He will deliver you out of all the challenges that you face in life and (2) if you're attempting to live a godly life, you should *expect* to go through your share of attacks.

If there were a person that was able to speak to us intimately about how to handle persecutions for the gospels sake, Paul would definitely be that person. Not only was he placed in jail for his beliefs, but if you would read II Corinthians 11: 25 & 26, you'd find out that Paul had been beaten with rods, stoned, suffered shipwrecks and suffered perils beyond what most of us would be able to stand, but as he testified in II Timothy 3, the Lord delivered him from them all. I believe that if GOD delivered Paul from all of his persecutions, He will definitely deliver you from all of your trials and tribulations as well! Your trials may pale in comparison to what Paul had to endure; yet regardless of how big or small, they do take a toll on your psyche. There are many people who are on the other side of their trials who can bear witness to the fact that GOD is able to deliver you through any and all things that may come your way. The key is for you to remain steadfast and unmovable, as well as be able to say like Job *"though He slay me, yet shall I trust Him."*

The second point that Paul makes in the above scripture is a reminder to some but news to others. It is a guarantee that once you begin doing anything for the kingdom of GOD, you should expect to be attacked in some way. Once you've decided that you will truly begin to transform your life and in the process stop doing some of the things that you use to do, such as hanging at "gentlemen's" clubs, drinking, cursing, or anything else that Satan used to keep you bound, that's when the devil turns up the heat and sends attacks your way to discourage you from living right. You weren't a threat to the devil when you were out there doing the things that you use to do. But as soon as you changed course and decided to transform your life by following Christ, you became his enemy and his job is to destroy you.

One of the keys to your new life and new walk in Christ is knowing what to expect in certain situations. Knowing what to expect will keep you from being surprised and taken back when things come your way, and it will allow you to be able to more effectively handle situations that will certainly come your way. Know that as you go about transforming your life and living your life for Christ, there will be tough times and times when the whole world seems to be against you. But that's alright because not only does Paul give us this guarantee but David has also told us in Psalms 34:19 that *"Many are the afflictions of the righteous but the Lord delivereth him from them all."* The dictionary defines "deliver" in many ways but the one that I like the most is *"to bring or transport to the proper place."* That's exactly what these scriptures are telling you about GOD. He will bring you to, not just "a" place, but to your "proper" place in life. It would mean nothing if I were suppose to deliver a package to 500 Madison Avenue but instead I took that package to 500 Fifth Avenue. Although I took that package to "a" place, I didn't take it to the "proper" place, so it's full value will not be realized. GOD wants to transport you from where you are to the place where He knows that He'll get the most out of you. But you first have to believe this. For you cannot receive it if you do not believe it!

Remember: Despite where you are in life, hold on, your "deliverer" is on the way!

Day 31

Life or Death…The Choice is Yours!

Read; Romans 8: 5 – 6
"For they that are after the flesh do mind the things of the flesh; but they that are after the Spirit the things of the Spirit.
For to be carnally minded is death; but to be spiritually minded is life and peace."

Over the last 30 days, I've attempted to share with you some of the things that GOD has revealed to me about transforming my life. One of the primary things that He showed me, and the main point that I tried to make in this book, is that in order for things to begin to change in our lives we must acquire a new mind about old issues. As Hebrews 12: 2 & 3 tells us, GOD wants us to guard ourselves mentally against all of the issues that surround us because, if we don't, we can become **"wearied and faint in our minds"**. Like I said in the beginning of this book, the only way things change is when we change the way we think about them. If you're overweight, the only way that situation will change is when you change the way you think about exercising and dieting. If you're living check to check, the only way that situation will change is when you begin to change you're thinking as it relates to spending and saving money.

GOD gave us very clear instructions regarding how to handle every situation in our lives. It's up to us to study the word and find the answers to our problems that He has "hidden" in the scriptures. You have to understand that the devil will do everything he possibly can to distract you with from getting this revelation. But GOD has been so good to us that He has given us a warning in His word regarding this attack as well. II Corinthians 11:3 tells us this: *"But I fear, lest by any means, as the serpent beguiled Eve through his subtlety, so your minds should be corrupted from the simplicity that is in Christ."*

My prayer is that the words that GOD has given to me regarding transformations and renewed minds has been helpful to at least one person who has read this. Over the last 30 days, I've touched on many different scriptures but the main point has been the same. Regardless of what you're going through, what you've experienced in your life, or how bad things may appear, GOD stands ready to deliver you from where you are to a predestined place of blessing both here on Earth and in Heaven. The choice is yours though; will you pay more attention to the things and problems that you can see, or will you begin to focus on GOD and His ability to change your situation? Psalms 23:7 tells us *"For as he thinketh in his heart, so is he."* If you think that you'll always be broke, you'll always be broke. If you think that things will never get better, they will never get better. I could just go on and on with this but I think you have the point. Regardless of how hard it will be at the beginning, start believing in your heart that you're going to come out of whatever situation that you're in and see how things begin to change in your life.

Remember: THINGS WILL CHANGE IN YOUR LIFE WHEN YOU CHANGE THE WAY YOU THINK ABOUT THEM!

Printed in the United States
145110LV00002B/1/A

9 780976 111207